Volume 1, American Indian Map-book Series

THE POMO INDIANS

OF CALIFORNIA

AND THEIR NEIGHBORS

By Vinson Brown

and

Douglas Andrews

Edited by Dr. Albert B. Elsasser

All illustrations in book and on map by Douglas Andrews,
except as indicated in acknowledgments.

NATUREGRAPH PRESS

619430

Naturegraph Publishers, Healdsburg, California 95448

SBN (paper) 911010-30-0
SBN (cloth) 911010-31-9

PREFACE

When Vinson Brown suggested that I might help him publish a map and book on the Pomo Indians and their neighbors, I thought I could be of little use in an enterprise that had really been completed long ago by anthropologists S. A. Barrett and A. L. Kroeber. On the other hand I realized that the maps showing the Pomo villages were out-of-print and virtually unavailable to great numbers of potentially interested persons. This being so, I consented to become a sort of copy reader and adviser on the few points of Pomo culture and geography with which I am familiar.

It requires not much more than a glance at the Pomo map for the thoughtful reader to become aware that here is really a brief but concentrated statement concerning the manner in which a people without agriculture occupied a fairly large part of aboriginal northern California. The Indians lived in this beautiful territory literally for thousands of years without spoiling it. If we think, however, that one of the reasons for this preservation was that they were merely wanderers and did not utilize the land very heavily, we are wrong, and the map is surely powerful evidence against us. The names on the map were all collected in the twentieth century, and together they serve as strong hints that the Indians were not unacquainted with any part of their wide terrain. Indeed they were apparently able to find something useful wherever they settled.

The text, with illustrations, which the authors have built around the map, provides in good measure what is, of course, demanded here, that is, some insight into how the Pomo peoples and their neighbors and ancestors lived, and how they managed to exploit their homelands so gracefully.

Albert B. Elsasser
R. H. Lowie Museum of Anthropology
University of California, Berkeley

DEDICATION

To all our Native Americans, and the completeness of their lives, their spirit and their joy.

TABLE OF CONTENTS

ACKNOWLEDGEMENTS

Although the bulk of the drawings in this book were done by Douglas Andrews, some were done by other artists to whom we owe our thanks. They include Mrs. Emily Reid, who did all the plant pictures on page 17; Rune Hapness of Norway, who did the fishes on the bottom of page 23; Donald Greame Kelley, who did pictures numbered 1, 2, 5, 6, 7, 9 and 10 on page 23, and reproduced here with the kind permission of Little, Brown and Co. of Boston from the book, The Amateur Naturalist's Handbook, by Vinson Brown; and Mrs. Carol Lyness, who did drawings numbered 3, 4, and 8 on page 23. We are especially grateful to Dr. Albert B. Elsasser of the Lowie Museum of Anthropology, University of California, Berkeley, who carefully read and edited the manuscript and proofs and gave great help with the illustrations. Another anthropologist, who read the proofs and gave fine help, was David Peri of Sonoma State College. The following Indians are much appreciated for their kind help with names and other matters: Pomo: Mrs. Elsie Allen, Mrs. Essie Parrish, Mr. Melvin Lucas, Mrs. Edna Guerero and Mr. Ralph Holder: Tuleyome: Mrs. Doris Yee. To the late Drs. S. A. Barrett and A. L. Kroeber of the University of California we owe deep appreciation for all their years of research that culminated in their and our map of the Pomo and their neighbors.

Essie Parrish (right) and Mable McKay are shown preserving Pomo basket-making techniques.   Photo courtesy Mrs. Parrish.

Giant Pomo storage basket being made at the Ukiah Rancheria in
1898. Photo by Nellie Burke, courtesy Mrs. Elsie Allen.

INTRODUCTION

This is the first of a series of maps and accompanying books on the major Indian tribes of North America, trying to put together in as illustrative and plain a way as possible the basic elements of the culture and religion of each. This we wish to do in a way that makes these people come alive so that we recognize them as flesh-and-blood human beings, using their intelligence and ingenuity to cope with their environment and having feelings of love and beauty and reverence that merit our respect and understanding. This may indeed be part of the great Tree of Understanding, foretold by Black Elk, the famous Sioux holy man, that would spread its branches over the world to bring all peoples together in unity under its healing shelter.

*Peter Farb classifies the Indians of America politically into:

      1. THE BAND
        a. The family
        b. The composite band
        c. The patrilocal band
      2. THE TRIBE
        a. The lineal tribe
        b. The composite tribe
      3. THE CHIEFDOM
      4. THE STATE

Most American Indians effectively acted in groups larger than the single family. Even where the social units were very small, as, for example, among the Shoshone Indians of Nevada, families which perhaps did not see each other for months would meet in a cooperative band for at least once in a year to gather a favorite crop or for ceremonies. In addition, other American Indians, such as the Aztecs and the Incas, had actual states, ruled by an elaborate governmental structure, and with great complexity in the use of material and social culture, so that one of the most ignorant judgments ever made has been to lump all American Indians together as uncivilized people.

Even the term "civilized" can have many meanings. If, by "civilized" we mean having many mechanical gadgets and comforts, then we are more civilized than any Indian peoples of the past. But if we mean people able to get along together in

---

* From the book MAN'S RISE TO CIVILIZATION AS SHOWN BY THE INDIANS OF NORTH AMERICA FROM PRIMEVAL TIMES TO THE COMING OF THE INDUSTRIAL STATE, by Peter Farb. Reprinted by permission of E. P. Dutton and Co., Inc.

comparative peace, with little or no war or crime, without a polluted atmosphere and water or other destruction of the environment, and with a close understanding between members of the society, then California Indians had a superior civilization.

The simple composite band of a few families gathering together for protection and food is found mainly among the desert peoples of California, but the Indians in the area of our map had patrilocal bands. This is because their social system was ruled by the fact that the small territory controlled by the band usually had plenty of both plant and animal food so that it was not necessary to travel far to find such food. Thus it was wise for the wife to move to her husband's family to live because he had special knowledge of the hunting territory, from being taught how and where to hunt in it from his own father (patrilocal lineage). Also, such a band, with its comparatively rich and constant food supply, had more leisure time to form a more elaborate religion and other specializations of culture.

The Pomo and all their neighbors had no such thing as a true tribe. The Pomo, for example, were simply groups of people with similar languages (some as far apart as French and English), who lived fairly close together, except for the Stony Creek or Northeastern Pomo (see map). Each band of Pomo usually had a small territory (rarely more than 20 miles wide) with a chief village where ceremonies were held, and one or more smaller villages surrounding it. Like most American Indians of old, each individual in this small territory was able to relate himself deeply to his environment, the woods, the waters, the rocks, the plants, the animals and birds and other creatures in a way that modern man has virtually forgotten, surely to his great loss. This is only one of the reasons why a study of these people and their interesting lives may be fruitful to us.

All these peoples, who, for so many thousands of years, were an intimate part of the nature of what is now Sonoma, Lake and Mendocino Counties, are now a submerged group in our massive and complex society and most have lost touch with the beautiful things their ancestors once knew. But more and more are now beginning to raise their heads with pride and seek knowledge and answers from and kinship with their vital past. If we can help them do this, we also will gain from the experience and become more graceful human beings.

DIVISION ONE - THE POMO

CHAPTER ONE - LANGUAGE, GENERAL CULTURE AND HISTORY

LANGUAGE

We should think of the Pomo not as a tribe, but as a cluster of bands or groups of people with similar languages in the same general geographical locality. This included most of what is now Sonoma, Lake and southern Mendocino Counties, but with a small offshoot over in Glenn County. Before white contact these language-related people never thought of themselves as a unit, but the invasion and interaction of whites gradually caused most of those who remained of the original groups to think of themselves as the Pomo, a name of an old-time Pomo village northwest of Ukiah.

The language is not too far from being as rich and complex as English, but is so different that it is hard for us to pronounce their words correctly and there are some words that are rich in many meanings because of changes in inflection. Some words that seem long to us may convey meanings that require several of our words, as, for example, Tcalámkiamali, meaning "to wind around a place on both sides village."

Pomo is not only divided into dialects but into what are actually separate languages. Thus an Eastern Pomo (see map) would probably find it as hard to understand a Southwestern Pomo as an Englishman would find it hard to understand a Dutchman! In listing some of the names and meanings of Pomo villages and some special locations in the back of this book, we realized it is exceedingly hard to be sure we were accurate because different anthropologists and different Pomo did not agree with each other on how to pronounce these names nor their meanings. Thus the list is only an approximation of what is the truth.

Pomo belongs to the Hokan linguistic family, which includes languages of great complexity and richness. It included the following other California linguistic groups: the Shastan, Chimariko, Yana, Karok, Washo, Esselen and Salinan of northern California, and the Chumash and Yuman (or Quechan) of southern California. Hokan forms a very old linguistic family in California, possibly the oldest of all and formerly very wide-spread.

GENERAL

The Pomo lived to the west of the heart of a unique cultural flowering of neighboring Indian peoples that rose during the last thousand years or so in what is now Central California west of the Sierras. It is called by anthropologists the "California Culture", as distinct from the "Northwest Coast Culture", which is renowned for its giant totem poles and the great ocean-going cedar canoes, or the "Pueblo Culture" of the southwest, noted for its apartment-houselike towns, constructed mainly from adobe bricks, and its complex, priesthood-dominated religion. Although the California Culture borrowed some elements from both of these areas, such as the sinew-backed bow from the northwest and, probably, the basic twined basketry from the southwest, it produced so many elements that were distinctively Californian that it can be thought of as a major culture center. Examples of such were the secret societies, with strikingly-dressed spirit impersonators, a part of the remarkable Kuksu Religion; the idea of a World Creator; beautiful feathered basketry; and a chief or leader whose special job was both to referee and to end battles and other frictions between groups and individuals.

In this cultural flowering three language groupings seem to have been most populous and so perhaps most active, at least in northern California. These were the Pomo on the north central California coast, the Wintun on the west side of the Sacramento Valley, and the Maidu, who lived east of the Sacramento River and up to the crest of the Sierras. Each of these had a unique and beautiful cultural development, much of which has unfortunately been lost. Something about the Wintun is given on page 55. The Californian Culture flourished most vigorously in the larger valleys, such as those of the Sacramento and Russian River, and around Clear Lake, where plenty of food, such as acorns, tubers, game and fish, gave more time for leisure activities. The mountain and hill Pomo, Wintun and Maidu, as well as surrounding hill peoples of other native stocks, had a harder struggle to keep alive. This probably made them more self-reliant and hardy, but gave them less time to develop specializations of culture. Nevertheless, their culture was complete on their own terms and mirrored very full and interesting lives.

We should realize that each tribal group or band lived within a small territory usually limited to one or two creeks and their watersheds. Beyond the surrounding hills there generally lived strangers, some of whom could be visited or who would come to visit after proper arrangements were made. But others might be hostile because of some misunderstanding or feud and so to be feared. Fifty miles away the world faded into a little known and finally formless vastness beyond the beyond.

SOME HIGHLIGHTS OF POMO HISTORY

Before the whites. Pomo history extends back for many thousands of years, but the recording of this history in legends and memorized stories was partly lost because of the indifference of the white man. The evidence is that the period was mainly a peaceful one, since the Indians of the area showed little organization for war.

1808. Russian and Aleut seal and sea otter hunters land at Bodega Bay, giving presents to local Olamentko (Coast Miwok).

1812. Founding of Fort Ross by Ivan F. Kuskoff, one-legged Russian adventurer, and first Commandant of the Fort.

1812-1847. From Fort Ross the Russians extended farms and trading out in various directions. This involved them with the local Pomo and Olamentko (Coast Miwok) Indians, whom they did much trading with and also used as laborers. At first they made allies of the Indians, as against a possible Spanish attack, were kind and friendly with them, married some of the women, and even supplied the Pomo with arms. Later some of the settlers stole children, shipping them to Russia, and relations deteriorated.

1823. Mission San Francisco Solano de Sonoma founded at present site of town of Sonoma by Father Jose Altimira. Franciscan fathers begin to gather converts (neophytes)from Pomo, Mayahk'mah (Wappo) and other native peoples. Flogging of Indians started, which begins much friction, and natives to the north threaten mission.

1834. General Mariano Vallejo secularizes the mission at Sonoma. He organizes friendly Suisun Indians under Sametoy (called Chief Solano) to help him fight Pomo and Miyahk'mah. Chief Saccara, of Healdsburg area Pomo, and his people rebel against Vallejo, and fight bravely, but are crushed by superior arms of Salvador Vallejo (brother of Mariano), and hundreds die.

1834-1847. Mariano and Salvador Vallejo ruthlessly carve out empire in Sonoma and Napa counties. They enslave Indians and Salvador treats the natives with extreme cruelty.

1848. Gold Rush brings miners and then American pioneers in numbers into Pomo country. A few Indians even join gold rush, but others are forced to help miners as virtual slaves. Granville P. Swift of the Sonoma Valley was a pioneer who enslaved Indians in this way, using chains and whippings.

1849. Stone-Kelsey ranchers near Clear Lake treat Pomo so badly that two Pomo cowboys, Shuk and Xasis, execute them. In revenge white army attacks innocent group of Pomo on island in Clear Lake, killing large number of men, women and children. Also other Pomo are attacked near Ukiah. Indian spirit is crushed by these massacres.

1870. Ghost Dance revival movement reaches Pomo. Medicine men from the Wintun come with story of Paiute prophet who says big wind will come after dance to destroy all white people. Indians in Clear Lake area build underground shelters to escape wind, and dance Ghost Dance. Ghost Dance discredited when wind does not come, and disheartened Pomo return to their homes. Southwestern Pomo have hard weary journey to their land by the sea and some die on the way, for they had come with high hopes to Clear Lake.

1870-1924. Pomo become a submerged people with little hope, working for white people at menial jobs, treated as second-class citizens, often not allowed in restaurants or theaters with whites. But the Pomo religion, now called Maru, and a combination of the old Kuksu religion with the adventist type Ghost Dance religion of 1870, continued with many of the Pomo, under the leadership of dreamer doctors, mainly women. Other Pomo become members of various Christian denominations. The Kashia, or Southwest Pomo, isolated in their hills, and least touched by white culture, are led by dreamer women doctors to maintain the old Pomo culture and religion to the greatest degree.

1904. A group of Yokaya Pomo (near Ukiah) win a court test and control over their own land when whites try to take it away from them.

1907. Ethan Anderson, a Pomo of Lake County, wins court test to allow a non-reservation Indian to vote.

1918. Society of Northern California Indians, including many Pomo, is organized to seek long-delayed justice.

1920. Pomo and other northern California Indians start court action to be paid for lands lost to the whites. This eventually leads to the California Indian Claims cases.

1968-1969. Pomo, helped by Ad-Hoc Committee on Indian Education, begin work to improve Indian education. From this come first plans to have multi-cultural approach to education in the schools of Mendocino and Sonoma Counties and the study of the Indian languages and culture.

CHAPTER TWO
DIVISIONS, HABITATS AND PHYSICAL CHARACTERS

What is difficult for the white people of California to understand or appreciate is that this state has been inhabited by Indians for at least 10,000 years, and the direct ancestors of the Pomo may have been among our oldest-known inhabitants. Generations of Pomo and their neighbors knew these lands so intimately that even single trees and rocks had rich meanings and bore special names. Our recent conquest of this land has brutally taken it away from an ancient people. Fathers, grandfathers and great grandfathers as far back as imagination cares to wander have enmeshed their feelings, thoughts and bones with the earth in a way we superficial newcomers can never equal.

The divisions of the Pomo can easily be seen in color on the map, but the kinds of habitats or living spaces inhabited by each and how it influenced them are given briefly below:

NORTHERN POMO - A coastal strip from just north of Navarro to a little past Fort Bragg is a region of low cliffs along the sea and with redwood forests just a few miles back. These were people who depended to a great extent upon the sea. They apparently avoided the great dark inland forests. The valley lands of the upper Russian River headwaters, the Navarro River Valley, and the upper parts of Outlet Creek near what is now Willits, were much more thickly populated and gave a richer life to the people who lived in valleys full of many good oak trees and other easily-taken food supplies. These people looked upon the acorn as their staple food. The northern Pomo over on the western edge of Clear Lake, at Blue Lakes and Tule Lake avoided the hills to the west and lived along the edges of the lakes where they combined acorns with fish and an abundance of other plant food. They went out on the lakes in tule balsas (rafts) and into the marshes for wild foods.

CENTRAL POMO - These people had a costal strip similar to that of their northern neighbors, a mountain and hill area around Yorkville and on the headwaters of the North Fork of the Gualala River, as well as a wide valley area along the Russian River where population and cultural sophistication also reached a high point. The mountain and hill people likewise avoided the redwood forests and sought areas near oak groves for their homes. The oaks were not as thick here as in the large valley to the east. Hence they had to depend more on hunting wildlife for food.

SOUTHERN POMO - Surprisingly the center of population and cultural elaboration of the southern Pomo was in the Russian River Valley around the present small town of Healdsburg, while the present populous center of Santa Rosa had few villages and few people. Perhaps the reason for this is that in those days Santa Rosa was an area of comparatively barren plain, while the rich, open forests and river near Healdsburg gave the Pomo there greater opportunities to secure food. Other parts of the Southern Pomo area were mountainous, with a few poor villages. A small area along the coast was enriched by sea food.

SOUTHWESTERN POMO - Since the territory of these people included largely dark, damp redwood forests and steep hills, the center of population and livelihood was largely along the edges of the sea and at the mouths of the streams where all kinds of marine life was hunted and collected. The hard work involved in gathering food prevented much elaboration of culture, but these people preserved much Pomo culture down to today.

EASTERN and SOUTHEASTERN POMO - These lake-shore peoples were dense in population because of the numerous wild foods of Clear Lake and its oak-covered shores.   The balsa raft or canoe (see page 28) greatly aided their food-getting.

NORTHEASTERN POMO - These adventurous but isolated people were concentrated along Stony Creek east of the main Coast Range, as most of their territory was mountainous and yielded little food. Though there were oaks along the creek, they had to work hard to live, hence their culture was not so elaborate as the Lake Pomo's. They had valuable salt-licks.

PHYSICAL CHARACTERISTICS OF THE POMO

The Pomo were of about medium height for California Indians.   They had broad faces and heads, comparatively narrow noses, and around 5' 5" average height for the men. Men were very strongly built, the women quite buxom, even in youth. A broad strong body, broad face, narrow nose and thin lips, were considered signs of handsomeness or beauty in these people.

In the old days the Pomo men were noted for their ability to carry a hundred pounds or more on their backs for long distances. The women showed great patience, concentration and skill in their weaving intricately-made baskets of all shapes and sizes. They could also pound away for hours at the job of making acorn meal or preparing other grains for food.

Pomo woman (Joseppa) holding basket full of army worms. June, 1904, in Ukiah Valley. Photo courtesy of Lowie Museum of Anthropology, University of California, Berkeley.

Pits filled with roasted grasshoppers around tree. Summer of 1903, Ukiah Valley. Photo courtesy of Lowie Mus. of Anthropology, University of California, Berkeley,

View of remains of Pomo fish dam, showing construction. One mile downstream from Calpella on Russian River. Photo by Dr. Barrett, courtesy Lowie Mus. of Anthropology, U. C., Berkeley.

Frame of Pomo summer house at northern end of Clear Lake, in 1901.   Photo by Goddard, couresy Lowie Museum of Anthropology, University of California, Berkeley.

CHAPTER THREE
MATERIAL CULTURE

Though the material culture of the Pomo was meager by our standards, they had developed many ways to make themselves comfortable, and to make life interesting by arts, crafts, games, dances and religious ceremonies. They were indeed far from being the crude savages early white Americans tried to picture them as in order to justify their conquest. Drawing their food directly from the land and its life, and gathering that food themselves, instead of from a supermarket, they knew every feature of their surroundings with a warm intimacy we would do well to envy. With the exception of a rare few genuinely interested in nature, the white child, woman or man today sees a wild plant, bird or animal with a blind indifference or ignorance that misses a hundred treasures of interest and knowledge known to every Pomo of old. (See pictures on pages 17 and 19.)

CHIEF PLANT FOODS

Women and children did most of the gathering of plant foods, though men occasionally helped, especially with the knocking down of pine nuts from the Digger Pines. A sharp-pointed stick of hard wood, such as madrone or mountain mahogany, was used for digging up tubers or roots and also for knocking edible seeds from bushes or grasses. A winnowing basket (shaped like a shallow dish) helped separate seeds from chaff. All foods found were generally carried home in a large back-basket.

Nuts and Seeds. The acorns, especially of the Black Oak, Tanbark Oak and Live Oak, were gathered in the fall. Part of the crop was stored in large storage baskets in huts. Those to be used soon, were ground with pestles in mortar baskets that were placed above hollows in hard anvil stones (see p. 25), then leached with water in a prepared basin of sand. The water, allowed to run over the acorn meal for some time, took out the bitter tannic acid. The leached meal was either boiled as mush in baskets with water and red-hot stones, or baked in ovens as bread. Ground buckeye balls were also leached, but much more thoroughly, often for months in running water, or buried in mud.

Some grass seeds, like those of the Chia, were gathered and roasted. Pine seeds of the Sugar Pine and Digger Pine were knocked out of the cones and then eaten either raw or roasted. Nuts of the California Bay were picked in the spring and then roasted and shelled to be pulverized for stored food for winter.

Bulbs of the soap plant were used both as soap and a fish poison, the pounded bulbs being thrown into calm water to stupify the fish for easy catching. But some of the interior Pomo baked the bulb to eat like a potato. Bulbs of the Brodiaea or Blue Dicks were eaten either raw or roasted.

Berries of some of the manzanitas were pulverized and mixed with water to eat or sometimes mixed with other foods for flavor. Lake Pomo made the berries into a drink. Toyon berries were heated in hot ashes and then eaten, but berries of the huckleberry, wild grape, western raspberry, wild strawberry, also the thimbleberry, etc., were eaten raw.

Ferns. Young curled tops of the bracken ferns were eaten raw, but also roasted for a day and night in hot ashes and then boiled. The root stocks were also boiled and eaten.

Tubers of the Arrowhead or Tule Potato were dug up in the marshes and either roasted or boiled, some being preserved after roasting for winter use.

Roots and Rootstocks. Rootstocks of the Yellow Pond Lily were dug up and baked, the seeds being used for bread or soup. The Squawroot or Yampah has roots that were gathered in spring, washed, trampled, then washed again, and cooked as potatoes are. One kind was boiled until mealy, peeled and cooked as a soup. Cowparsnip roots were cooked like rutabaga.

Leaves of such plants as Miner's Lettuce, early spring Cowparsnip, and some clovers, etc. were eaten raw. Others, such as the leaves of some lupines, Hedge Mustard, goosefoots, etc., were boiled in baskets with hot stones and water like spinach.

Flowers of some plants, such as clovers, mallows, etc. were eaten raw.

Sugar was made by cutting bark of Sugar Pine and gathering the sweet sap when it solidified.

Salt was usually obtained from seaweed on the coast, or from saltlicks in the interior.

Seaweed of several species was dried on rocks and then taken home to be stored and then cooked later in earth ovens, then made into cakes. Sea Palms were cooked in hot ashes or on a flat rock. Kelp was also cooked in hot ashes.

Gum was made from pine pitch.

Many other plants were used, not only for food, but also for medicine, but this will give some idea of the variety.

Bracken Fern

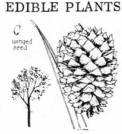

Digger Pine

Arrowroot (tule potato)

Coast Live Oak

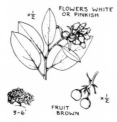

Hoary Manzanita

California Bay

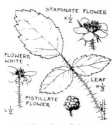

Wild Blackberry

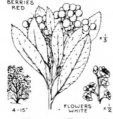

Toyon Berry

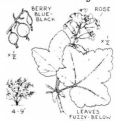

Wild Currant

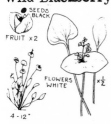

Miner's Lettuce

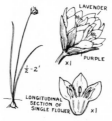

Blue Dicks

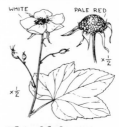

Thimbleberry

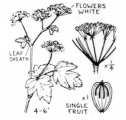

Cow Parsnip

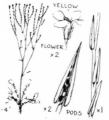

Hedge Mustard

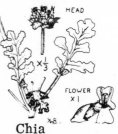

Chia

ANIMAL FOOD, HUNTING AND TRAPPING (typical animals hunted are shown on page 19, hunting and trapping equipment are shown on page 21).

Elk were shot with bows and arrows or surrounded by a large ring of hunters and killed with spears. These large animals were hard to kill and took strenuous efforts with much excitement and danger, especially from the bulls or cows with calves.

Deer were sometimes surrounded also, but were more often hunted by men who were specially trained and equipped to approach deer, disguised as buck deer wearing head and horns of killed animal (see color picture on map). The deer was approached with great caution, the hunter pretending to act like a feeding deer until near enough to use bow and arrow. Deer were also trapped in nooses strung along deer trails (see p. 21), or in nets. Both nooses and nets were made of very strong plant materials (such as the withes of Virgin's Bower) in order to hold such a large and struggling animal. Both elk and deer meat was smoked over a slow fire in large quantities to preserve it for future use, especially during the winter. The skins of both deer and elk were used in clothing and bedding.

Bears, especially grizzly bears, were rather rarely hunted because of the danger from them. However, some groups of Pomo did hunt bears, especially for the skins, while others avoided them almost entirely. When hunted, bears were either surrounded and speared, or killed by a powerful man with bow and arrow.

Mountain lions, at least in some areas, were prized for both meat and skins. A good hunter might get one by stalking with bow and arrow. It was difficult to get close enough for a spear.

Sea lions and seals (usually the harbor seal), were either reached by powerful swimmers swimming out to off-shore rocks along the coast, or by men riding log rafts out to the rocks in good weather. Generally these animals were killed by clubbing them to death, and the bodies then dragged by ropes behind the swimmers or the rafts back to the land where they were skinned and the meat cut up for cooking.

Sea otters were prized for their fine fur on some parts of the coast and ignored on others. Usually only chiefs were rich enough to buy such furs, which might be used as a badge of rank. These animals also were clubbed to death on the rocks or were harpooned with harpoons having detachable heads. (See p. 24.)

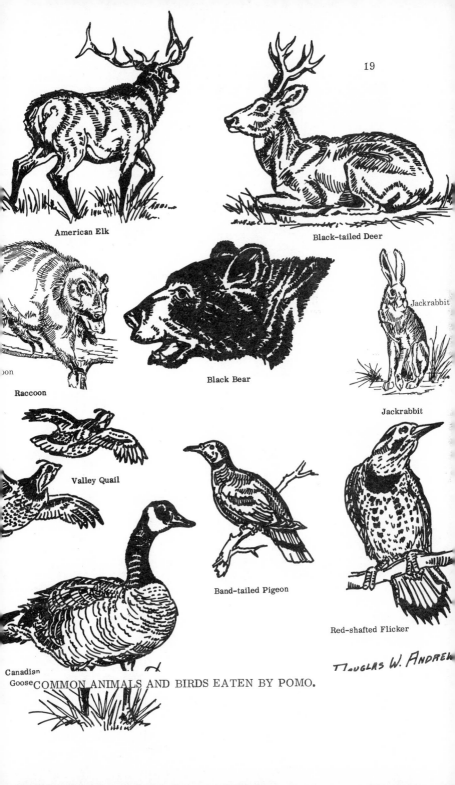

American Elk

Black-tailed Deer

19

Raccoon

Black Bear

Jackrabbit

Jackrabbit

Valley Quail

Band-tailed Pigeon

Red-shafted Flicker

Canadian Goose

Douglas W. Andrew

COMMON ANIMALS AND BIRDS EATEN BY POMO.

Brush rabbits, cottontails and jackrabbits (hares) were most often trapped by snares set in their trails among the bushes, speared with sharp sticks, or killed with slings and arrows.

Boys would try to surround jackrabbits in practice for the way men would surround deer.   Blankets were often made out of twisted rabbit fur and were warm and serviceable.

Squirrels were usually shot out of trees with arrows.   Like most small mammals, they were usually crushed before cooking.   Boys chased down ground squirrels and killed with sticks.

Wood Rats were flushed by tearing up their nests, chased up bushes and knocked out of them with sticks.

Many birds were hunted and trapped, including especially:

Valley and Mountain Quail.   These were hunted with blunt arrows to stun them.   A favorite way was to build brush walls in the form of a V, the birds being driven toward the point of the V where a hunter or hunters would be waiting.   Quail traps were made out of open-work basketry with a large opening in which the bird entered and a small end where it would become imprisoned. Often the Pomo used quail traps as much as twenty-five feet in length (see picture on page 21).   Since quail almost always moved uphill, a trap was set on such a slope, and the Indians very slowly and cautiously drove the birds uphill into it.

Woodpeckers were needed for their bright feathers, used in dance costumes and prize baskets, but were also eaten.   They too were trapped in similar round, narrowing basket-work traps put up in trees, or their calls were imitated to attract them and then they were shot with bows and arrows.

The Band-tailed Pigeon and Sooty Grouse were often knocked out of the branches of trees where they slept at night. Most bird meat also was pounded to pieces before cooking in the ovens.

Ducks and wild geese were hunted in the marshes, by the aid of decoys and with bows and arrows, or sometimes trapped in nets when they lighted on the waters.   Clear Lake was especially noted for great flocks of them and fine hunting.

Turtles were the most common reptiles eaten, usually being cooked in hot ashes.   Small lizards were also eaten.

Grasshoppers were trapped in a ring of fire in dry grass, which also cooked them, then eaten soon after.

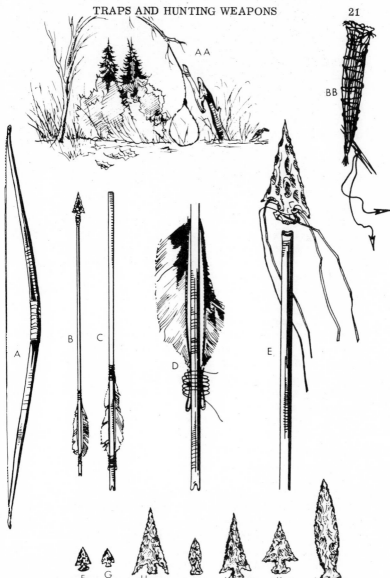

TRAPS AND HUNTING WEAPONS: AA. Typical noose snare, BB. trap for quail, placed in trail through brush so quail enters and gets stuck in narrow end; A. sinew-backed bow; B. hunting arrow; C. detail of feathers on shaft; D. same enlarged; E. head of spear ready for attachment; F-L. arrowhead and spear points.

FISH, FISHING AND SEA FOODS

While considerable fishing was done by the Pomo along the rivers, such as the Russian and the Gualala, and off the rocks of the ocean shore, this profession reached its greatest complexity and perfection among the Clear Lake Pomo, who extensively used the rafts made out of bound tules (see p. 28), and developed elaborate nets and fish traps. At Clear Lake, also, fishing was more clearly a specialized profession where certain men did nothing but fishing and traded their catch for other things they needed. Often they fished all night when the fish fed.

Fish hooks were used mainly on the lake or on the ocean shore, and were made out of shell or bone. Most stream fishing was done by spearing or by nets or weirs. A weir was made by running two brush and stick fences in the water to a narrow opening where fish could be driven and then caught with the hands. Poisoning was done in still or semi-still water by dropping ground-up soap plant bulbs or buckeye balls into the water, poisonous substances in them stupefying the fish so they could be caught on the surface easily.

The fish spear was usually three pronged with horn or bone points lashed to the shaft, though sometimes sharp obsidian was used. The harpoon, used mainly at the lake, had two or three prongs, and was made of two parts, the lower with the prongs being detachable, so that a large fish, like a salmon or big steelhead, would carry off the head of the harpoon attached by a cord to the main shaft. (See page 24.)

Seine nets were used by several boatmen on the lake to surround schools of fish. Stretched gill nets were tied to stick posts in the shallows. Smaller gill nets helped land the fish.

Fish were mainly grilled over fires or baked in the oven. They were also dried and smoked for a reserve food supply.

Ocean fish were caught mainly near the beach with hooks and lines. The octopus was taken with fish poison from its cave or speared in the tide pools. The tentacles only were baked in an earth oven. Abalone was very popular and was dried raw, then cooked in long strips on hot coals in the earth oven, or sometimes allowed to soften before cooking or beaten to softness. Chitons were scraped free of inedible parts and baked over coals in the earth oven. Barnacles were cooked in hot sand that was mixed with red-hot coals. They were also dried, as were chitons, in the sun and stored for the future.

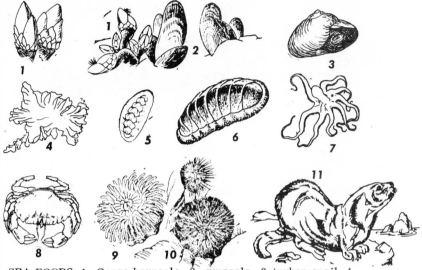

SEA FOODS: 1. Goose barnacle, 2. mussels, 3. turban snail, 4. ruffled purple rock weed, 5. lined chiton, 6. mossy chiton, 7. octopus, 8. cancer crab, 9. sea anemone, 10. sea urchins, and 11. sea otter (mainly killed for the warm and beautiful fur).

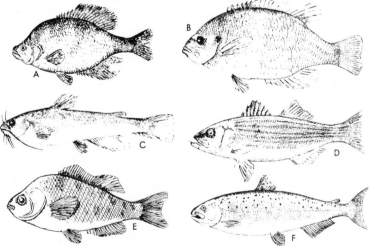

FISH OF STREAMS AND LAKES: A. White crappie, B. green sunfish, C. square-tailed catfish or brown bullhead, D. striped bass, E. fresh water live bearing perch, F. king salmon.

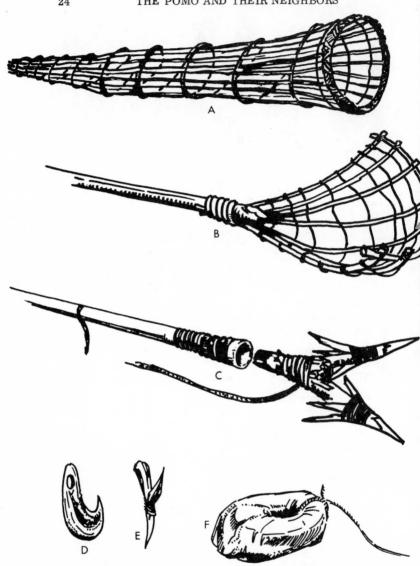

FISHING TOOLS: A. Basket fish trap; fish swims in large end and gets trapped in small end or swims into other basket trap; B. scoop net for scooping fish out of water; C. harpoon with detachable head for spearing large fish; points usually made out of bone; D. curved hook; E. tied hook, made out of bone; F. fishing charm.

AIDS TO COOKING: **A.** 2 long stirring spoons, as occasionally used to place hot rock in water-tight basket to boil water; **B.** underground oven, using hot rocks and ashes around leaf-wrapped food; **C.** mortar basket with acorn meal placed in hole in rock to be pounded; **D.** stone mortar and pestle, often used by old people to grind food finer than usual to assist digestion; **E.** rush mat with acorns piled on it before grinding; **F.** soft stone bowl used to hold pitch, etc. ; **G.** Pomo woman grinding acorns with pestle.

VARIOUS TOOLS AND THEIR USES

The Pomo had numerous tools for daily use, far more than we can picture or describe here. Here are some common ones:

Bones, horns, hard woods and various kinds of rock, but particularly obsidian, were used in the making of tools and the Pomo developed many clever ways to make and use them.

Bone or horn awl. The bone was sharpened by grinding to a sharp point, and fashioned so it could be easily gripped in one hand while puncturing holes in skins or wood, and so forth.

Bone or horn knife. This kind of knife was much more common than the obsidian kinfe, which was harder to make. The bone or horn could be shaped better by grinding and a good handle fashioned quickly. Used for carving meat, eating, cutting.

Fire drill. In the old days the Pomo twirled a drill to produce fire only by using the hands. The drill was usually made of a straight stick from a wild currant bush, while the wood drilled to produce friction, heat and fire was usually dried buckeye. A handful of mouse nest or other fine dry material was used as tinder, and the first spark was blown into flame. Some Pomo struck two pieces of white quartz together to make sparks.

The arrow straightener. Arrows, after being scraped to proper thickness and dried, were separated into two piles, one of straight and the other of crooked. A crooked arrow was put into a hole previously ground through a flat slab of soap stone about five inches long, which had previously been well-heated in fire. Water dropped on the wood caused it to steam and the fibers relax so the crooked part straightened as it cooled.

Elk horn wedge. A thick piece of elk horn was ground into a sharp wedge. This was used for splitting wood for firewood or making rough posts out of logs with easily split grain to use in building houses. Wooden slabs for trays were also split out.

Maul stone. This was a stone hammer without a handle.

Obsidian flaker of elk horn. This tool had a sharp point which was pressed against a piece of obsidian, as shown, with sufficient sudden force to break off a flake. Much experience, care and patience was needed to produce good stone knives, arrowheads or spearheads. Many were broken before finishing.

Drill with stone point. A small obsidian point was fastened with sinew to a straight piece of hard wood and used for drilling wood, bone, horn, shell or soft soapstone. The drill stick was held between the two hands and twirled back and forth by brisk rubbing while applying as much pressure as possible.

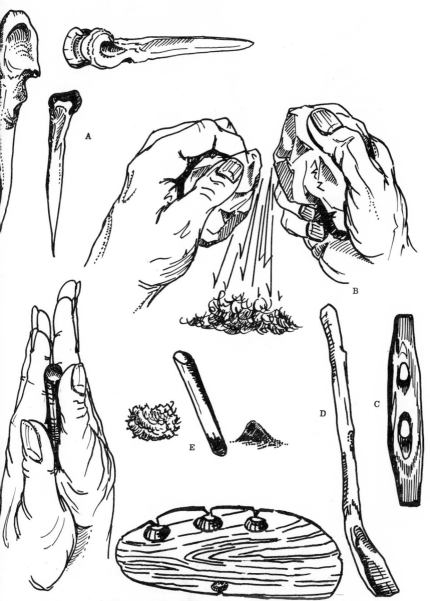

VARIOUS TOOLS: A. bone awls; B. making fire with two quartz stones; C. stone arrow straightener; arrows held in holes after steaming and bent straight; D. stirring spoon; E. fire-making outfit of dried buckeye wood base, ash or pine twirling stick and mouse-nest tinder; F. stick twirled rapidly in hands for friction.

NAVIGATION

The bound rush boat or balsa canoe, illustrated in color on the map and in black and white on this page, was the crowning instrument of Pomo navigation. It was really a raft shaped out of the tule rushes, as it did not depend, as does the ordinary boat, on keeping the water out of the center to stay on top of the water. The rushes themselves were hollow and so kept it afloat even when water came up through them. They were bound tightly together, usually with grape vine. Crude, quickly-made balsas were put together for crossing rivers, but on Clear Lake, the Pomo learned to shape their balsas beautifully, with raised-up sides, well-pointed and raised prows, and other helps such as seats. In shallow waters it was generally moved with a long pole, but on the lake a single paddle with a broad and short blade was used, and it could be driven with a fair speed because of its lightness, especially when the water was calm.

The normal population of Pomo around Clear Lake was comparatively numerous because of a plentiful food supply and we can imagine that lake full of moving or stationary fishing balsa canoes on some warm summer evening of the long-ago. Merry were the shouts of the children, trailing their hands in the water, where families went out together, and deeper the cries of the men asking about the catches of fish.

The ocean waves did not allow the frail balsas to be used on the Pacific coast, but temporary rafts made out of large pieces of redwood driftwood were sometimes tied together so Indians could go out to nearby seal rocks. To reach rocks a mile or more out, the seal hunters usually swam, carrying clubs to kill seals and a rope to tow the dead bodies back to the land with. It is likely that large baskets were used to ferry small children across the rivers, a swimmer pushing the basket.

Pomo in rush balsa canoe on Clear Lake about 1890.   Photo courtesy of Southwest Museum, Los Angeles, California.

Pomo village near Clear Lake about 1890.   Boards have been
used in some houses.   Photo courtesy of Bancroft Library, University of California, Berkeley.

Ruins of summer sweat house, showing framework, at Beattie
Rancheria in Russian River Valley, 1901. Photo by P. E. Goddard
and courtesy of Lowie Mus. of Anthropology, U. C., Berkeley.

1, Center post; 2, 3, outer &
inner doors; 4, firewood; 5 the
fire; 6, drum; emergency ex-
it; A, ash ghost performers;C,
chief; D, drummer; E, fire ten-
ders; M, master of ceremonies;
RR dancers; SS singers; X-Y,
visitors; Y-4, home people.

POMO BUILDINGS: A. Family house with framework of willow
saplings, thatched with tules and other leaves; B. summer brush
hut with skin door; C. dance house with floor about three feet underground; similar in appearance to smaller sweathouse; D. a
dance house constructed above ground with boards fairly recently; E. Pomo Redwood Tipi; F. diagram of dance house and par-
ticipants in operation (after Barrett).

HOUSES AND OTHER BUILDINGS

Large and rather comfortable houses were built in the valleys, but the hill people built smaller structures.   Permanent dwellings were generally put up along streams for living during winter and spring, while the temporary shelters were put up in hills on treks for food during the drier weather.   But hilltops were used for permanent villages in damper forest areas.

Bark tipi.   This was generally built by the coastal people who could get thick slabs of bark from the nearby redwood trees with the aid of elk-horn wedges. A central pole, usually with a forked top, was put up, and long willow or other young tree trunks leaned against it. Against this were piled the redwood bark slabs until all holes were covered except a smoke hole in the top and a small doorway down below.

Brush house. This was the common round or oval community dwelling of the valleys, which was sometimes as much as 40-50 feet in diameter.   A frame of willows was constructed and curved in toward the central roof hole, the frame then being covered thickly with brush and foliage.   Several families had their sleeping quarters around the interior, with a central space reserved for all to cook in.   There were usually two doors. The beds were made of mats of grass or tules laid on the ground, or sometimes placed on raised platforms.

Sweat house. This was a smaller, circular house, constructed in a similar way, except a pit a foot or more deep was dug first and dirt piled on top of the brush roof.   Only men were usually allowed in this house (except an occasional old woman), in which a fire or red-hot stones were used to start a profuse sweating. In cold weather the men often slept here.   Also the sweat house was often used as a club house for discussion of men's affairs.

Dance or Ceremonial House.   This was built like the sweat house in a circle, often over a shallow excavation, and with dirt piled on top of the brush roof.   But it was usually much larger, sometimes 70 feet wide, with 2 doors, and a smoke hole (see diagram of inside on page 30). Usually the doors were at the beginning of passageways leading into the big room. Leaves and small branches of trees were spread around the outer parts of the circular room for the spectators to sit on. In some areas, especially the north, plants were used in the walls.

Temporary structures. In summer the valley people often moved into the cooler hills, where they lived in temporary lean-tos or under brush shelters made mainly to keep out the sun.

CLOTHING AND CARRYING EQUIPMENT

The clothing ranged from nothing at all, customary with many men in warm weather, to elaborate dance costumes of skins, reed breast plates, hair nets and brilliantly feathered head-dresses.   The ordinary clothing of the man in cool weather was a blanket of twined and woven rabbit skins, with thrust-through holes for the arms and a rope sash to tie it about the middle if needed. No hat was worn, but, if cold enough, low sewn skin moccasins were put on the feet. Wealthier men and chiefs were inclined to wear seal skin or even sea otter skin blankets. A loin cloth of deer or other skin was occasionally but not often worn or a skin was simply wrapped and tied about the hips. Men usually made the dance costumes for both men and women, of which a typical one is shown in full color on the map. . Flicker feathers were used in the head band, which is shown unusually tall in the picture. Such costumes were extremely varied and colorful, decorated with both beads and feathers in many intri-cate designs, showing talented artistic ability.   It is very sad that these magnificent costumes are so rarely seen these days. We should encourage the Pomo to bring back the great dances of old, as they show a unique and beautiful flowering of culture and have rich spiritual meanings.

The women wore a two piece skirt of skin or strips of tule or other plant fibers or both plant fibers and skin in combination, with a narrow apron-like part in front and a wider hind section covering clear around the hips.   In younger women some skin was usually raised to cover the breasts. Women usually wore a rabbit-skin blanket around their shoulders in cold weather. A skin skirt often was slit along the bottom for decoration and for greater freedom of movement.

A basket cradle was carried on the back by a mother with a baby. It was a great aid to the mother in allowing her arms to be free to work. Diaper material was usually made out of soft shredded bark. A rabbit-skin blanket was wrapped around the baby to keep it warm in cold weather and it was lashed into place with rawhide thongs. This probably helped develop an erect way of walking and a straight back.

Both men and women used large carrying baskets with head straps to carry things on journeys, but the women did almost all the carrying on lesser trips. It was very remarkable how even old people carried immense loads gracefully and tirelessly.

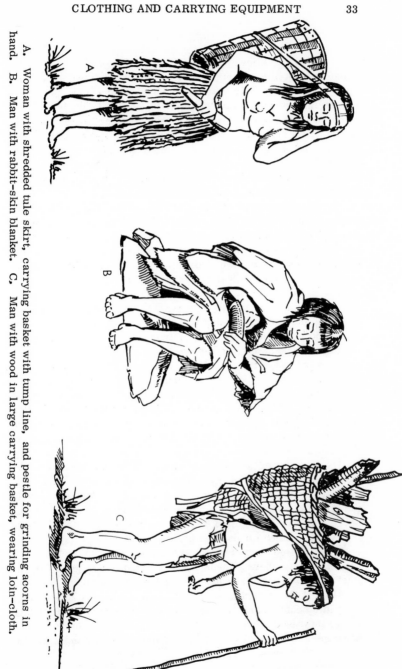

A. Woman with shredded tule skirt, carrying basket with tump line, and pestle for grinding acorns in hand. B. Man with rabbit-skin blanket. C. Man with wood in large carrying basket, wearing loin-cloth.

BASKETRY

Basketry is believed by many scientists to have reached its greatest peak of achievement in America among the Pomo. This speaks highly of their artistic and inventive genius, but sadly of our lack of understanding of their aesthetic ideals, for few Pomo baskets are now made and basket-making of this high quality may be a dying art. Recently some basketry has been shown and classes of the technique held among the Pomo and for some white women in Ukiah and at the Kashia Rancheria near Stewart's Point, but this kind of interest will only flicker and die out unless it is continually encouraged.

The two main types of woven baskets, twined and coiled, are shown in the pictures on page 35.   Twined basketry is found among Indian peoples to the north of the Pomo and coiled basketry is far commoner among natives to the south, but the Pomo uniquely combined the two kinds of basketry in an infinite variety of ways and always with superior techniques.

The twined baskets, however, are generally made for rougher usage, such as for holding acorns when they are pounded, back pack baskets and for packing freshly-gathered acorns.   But the Pomo did have almost every variety of twining, including lattice twining, checkerwork, and so on.

In coiled basketry, they had both single-rod and double-rod coils, and used on both these kinds of baskets many elaborate decorations of brilliantly-colored feathers, beads and shells (as shown in color on the map). So tightly were these baskets often put together that they could hold water without leaking.   Red hot stones dropped into such a basket full of meal and water gradually could bring the mixture to a boil and thus cook mush.

The Pomo used as many as twelve different materials for making baskets, but the chief ones were the willow, used universally as the warp in either twined or coiled basketry; while the following four were common as the woof: (1) the root of the sedge (used in both coiled and twined basketry; (2) the bark of the redbud, which furnished a beautiful red pattern; (3) the bulrush root, often dyed black to give a black pattern; and (4) Digger Pine root fibers, which are very strong and good for the woof in twined baskets that were used for rough wear.

All of these materials have become much harder to get since the white people came, as the Indians have been kept out of land where they used to go in the old days to find these things.   We can hope that more land-owners will help to renew this fine art.

Pomo basket-maker of Ukiah Rancheria, showing beginning of work on coiled basket. Courtesy Mus. of Anthropology, U. C.

POMO BASKETS: A. Mortar basket for placing on rock grinding basin; B. old picture of feather basket (courtesy Bancroft Library); C. basket cup; D. twined carrying basket; E. water-tight and coiled basket such as used for boiling water.

The Indians are actually very careful to preserve these plants that are so useful to their basket-making and use only what is actually needed without destroying too much. It is, therefore, vital for more white people to offer the opportunity to Indians to find these plants on their lands if this beautiful work is to be preserved and encouraged. One of the authors of this book helped Mrs. Elsie Allen, a Pomo basket-maker of Ukiah, find a ranch whose owner allowed the gathering of fine sedge roots.

The sedge roots are dug up very carefully so as to make them as long as possible, dried, and then split down the middle. They are hung up to dry for about a year. Slender willow shoots are selected from trees in the springtime, with different sizes for different kinds of baskets. Each shoot must be stripped of bark and then whittled down to make it even in size. It is dried for a few days in the hot sun, and then each size sorted and hung in a dry place for about a year.

It may take as much as two months to make a fine basket, which explains why the price on such a basket often sounds too high to the buyer. To begin a single stick coil basket, two roots of sedge grass are knotted together, then one willow added at a time, coiling the sedge root tightly around each willow so as to completely hide the willow as the basket is made. An awl is used to force a space between each coil of a root and the willow, making it easier to coil the root around the willow. The top of the basket is usually evened off with a willow coiled about it and then wrapped with sedge root. To explain fully how to make baskets of the various types would take a separate book. Here we can give only an inkling.

The highly decorated baskets, especially the feather ones, were usually prestige items, often given as presents to leaders and kept as family heirlooms. Some were quite literally considered beyond value and were never sold. Unfortunately some unscrupulous white men threatened and frightened some Pomo basketmakers into selling their work to them at unfair prices, and much harm was done. Today we need to overcome this by setting prices on this art which correspond with the hard work and exquisite sense of beauty that is involved.

CHAPTER FOUR
SOCIAL AND RELIGIOUS CULTURE

SOCIAL ORGANIZATION

General

On the surface, if we were to go back to the old days, the social organization of the Pomo would appear very loose and simple, close to what we might call anarchy. But a really complicated system of religious and psychological incentives and curbs to conduct underlay this seeming simplicity and functioned to make things we take for granted in our society, such as police, courts, government structure (except in the simplest possible form), and so forth, generally unnecessary.

It is true that families had joined together to form villages and a few villages usually cooperated enough to form the largest Pomo political unit, the tribelet or band. This was generally made up of a few small villages clustered around one large village where religious ceremonies and larger social events usually were centered. In this larger village the head chief held sway, while lesser villages had lesser chiefs. These chiefs, and the headmen of the families, who were next under them in control of the people, were usually hereditary but had to prove themselves as good leaders or forfeit the job by social pressure. Their proof of this character was usually a dignified demeanor, courage and stoicism under pressure or emergency, wisdom in handling other people and an upright conduct. They had little direct power, such as giving orders, except sometimes in emergency, but many became clever diplomats, speakers, persuaders and users of astute psychology, so having great influence. The chief's principal functions were to bring peace between quarrelling families or villages, organize food-gathering or trading expeditions, help direct ceremonies, and exhort the people to lead more cooperative and productive lives. Most were good orators. Men did not usually become regular or "men chiefs" until they were fairly old and experienced. "Boy chiefs", who might be men of forty or more, were in line of succession to become "men chiefs" by heredity, but had to prove themselves by taking on lesser jobs, like hunting expeditions or trading trips.

The individual's life actually centered around the family, and strong families had good headmen, good cohesion and cooperation, good moral conduct, and several men and women who were experts or professionals in such lines as fishing or basketry.

Some Social Actions and Instruments of the Pomo.

The Pomo had far more social abilities than can be told about here and were a richly-endowed people. Some were:

Music and musical instruments. In the old days the Pomo were always singing songs of both religious and social significance. The young man usually sang a song to the girl he loved and hoped she would hear it. The mother sang many lullabies to her baby. Men sang songs for hunting, fishing and the like.

Musical instruments included, among others: (1) the flute, made out of an elderberry stick about 10 inches long, with mouth holes at each end and four note holes in four segments in the middle. This was often used by the young man to court his girl; (2) three kinds of whistles, including the one-bone whistle, the two-bone whistle and the large Kuksu whistle, made out of elderberry wood and used in religious ceremonies; (3) two kinds of rattles, one made out of split elder wood (as shown), bound and painted and used as a clapper in dancing, and the other out of 6 cocoons, filled with little pebbles, bound with skin, and hung from a long stick with strings, to be used in dances and in curing by medicine men; (4) the hollow log drum, without any skin over the ends, supported on posts with ropes and tramped on or thumped with a thick stick to make a hollow sound at the dances; and (5) the musical bow, just for amusement.

Money. The Pomo made most of their money out of the Washington Clam, found mainly at Bodega Bay, and so traded for with the Olamentko. The clam was cut in pieces, drilled for beads and ground round and smooth on stones. The beads were placed on necklace strings of usually 200 beads. Long, cylindrical beads, made from the thickest part of the shell, were the most valuable, worth 20 to 40 times as much. Far more valuable, worth 2000 to 4000 shell beads (or possibly $5.00 each), were beautiful cylindrical beads made out of cooked magnesite ore (found to the east of Clear Lake). These were not only carefully drilled and shaped, but polished first against stone, and then rubbed in the hands for years to increase their value.

Gambling. There were several different forms of gambling, but the most prevalent was called the Grass Game. Two or more on a side played at this for hours, singing all the time to distract the opponents, a player with special sticks handling and hiding them under a pile of grass, until calling on the opponents to guess where the sticks were hidden. A good guess brought a shout of triumph and an exchange of money, a poor one jeers!

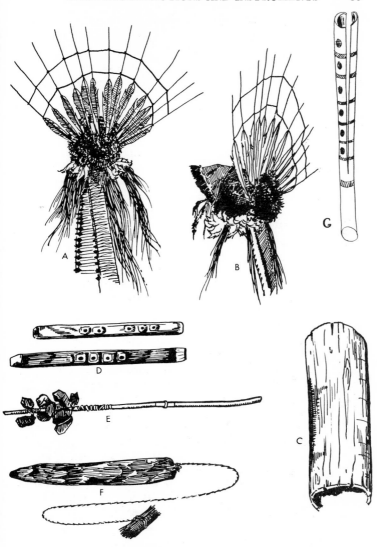

A. Dance headpiece with large tail feathers on top and 2 flicker feather bands, seen from in back; B. same, side view; C. large log drum without covered ends; D. two elderberry flutes; E. rattle made of cocoons and stick; F. bull-roarer, swung around the head to produce roaring noise and frighten and awe women and children at time of night ceremonies; G. elderberry dance clapper.

Counting, time and astronomy. The Pomo showed great arith-
metical skill in being able to count as high as 40,000. They used
beads and different sized sticks laid out on smooth ground to do
this, counting in multiples of tens as we do. They had specialists
who kept count of dates, months, seasons and years, sometimes
with markings on rocks or carved sticks. These men might also act as historians, recounting great events by aid of their
markers and giving exact times. They named some of the bright
stars and constellations and, of course, had stories about them.

Games. After a time of good harvesting of wild crops and
wild animal foods, the people had leisure for games. The chief
men's game was something very like our hockey, using a hard
wood ball and hitting it with curved sticks to drive it through a
goal, usually made of posts. There was much yelling and
screaming at this game from both players and spectators.

Women had a game in which they used six split sticks that
were flat on one side and round on the other. Three were
marked and three unmarked. The women threw them in special
ways and then guessed where the marked ones were.

Children had many games. One was like jack-stones, throwing up a stone instead of a ball, but picking things up while the
stone was in the air. Cat's cradle with string made out of plant
fibers was also played. The springing stick game was fun for
both girls and boys, as sticks made out of springy wood were
stuck in the ground and then pulled back and let go so they would
fly through the air. The one that went farthest won.

Of course tag was a popular game, as was hide-and-seek,
but circle kick ball usually had everybody in stitches of laughter!
The children formed a circle and then kicked a ball made out of
tightly-bound skins around the circle. Any boy or girl who
missed in kicking or kicked too far, had to leave the circle.

Girls, of course, made dolls out of pieces of wood or stuffed
skins and played house. A real prize was to have a mother make
a little doll-carrying basket that the girl-mother could carry her
doll with on her back. They also "baked" bread with mud or clay.

Boys twirled tops made of acorns or sticks. But many games
were simply copying hunting or other activities of the men. A
favorite was arrow-throwing with pointed sticks about 3 feet long
by 3/4 inches thick. The arrows, as spears, were thrown so they
would glance off the top of a mound and then spring farther
through the air. Arrows that went farthest won. This game had
its rough part, for the loser had his elbow struck and could not cry!

Trade and Trails

The stockily-built Pomo men were noted for their ability to carry up to 200 pounds in pack baskets with a tump line over the forehead.   Trade and visiting were carried out over the trails shown on the map and others we don't know about. Men were so used to long-distance walking that they travelled over these trails with a kind of graceful ease, even when under heavy packs, that really ate up the long miles.

Many of the inland people moved down to the sea on trips every summer to gather seaweed and salt, as well as sea food, usually by permission of the coast tribelets. Also great summer trading expeditions were made for many miles into the lands of neighboring peoples, always by permission of these neighbors. Seashells and dried sea foods were thus carried inland to the Lake Pomo and other interior peoples by the coastal Pomo. So sinew-backed yew bows came down from the Yuki and other northern peoples, along with bear skins and bright red pileated woodpecker feathers, to be traded for magnesite bead money, seashells and fine baskets, or obsidian knives and arrowheads taken from the black obsidian deposits of Mt. Konocti.

The trails usually followed the ridges where there were canyons and along the rivers in the large valleys. Sometimes all the villagers left home to cross the mountains to Clear Lake or down the river to the ocean to trade or feast.   These were usually joyous and exciting occasions, especially for the children, who must have run all about the edges of the caravan, seeing the new sights of new country and being shrilly called back when they wandered too far! For example, the people of Komli, in the Russian River Valley, might put together most of their shell money and good baskets and come over to Noberol on the west side of Clear Lake to trade money and baskets for a big feast of cooked lake fish. Such a social get-together might last for several days. At such times everybody would have a big time, dance and sing, laugh and play games, and many a marriage for young people might be contracted between families, or sometimes a pair, whose parents disapproved, would elope.

Such gatherings were usually arranged long ahead of time, first at a council of the head men with the chief, and then by messenger calling on a distant village and asking for a chance to visit and trade, or sending an invitation to come and trade to the distant village. Marked sticks gave the date when to come.

Warfare.

The fact that the Hokan-speaking peoples, of whom the Pomo are one branch, once extended over most of California, while peoples of such languages as the Penutian Miwok and Wintun came later, makes it likely that these later people were invaders who pushed the Pomo into the area where they were found by the white people. If so, there may have been a time of extensive warfare some thousand or so years ago when the newcomers came. However, in more recent centuries, but before the whites came, it is evident that the Pomo had little major warfare because their social system shows little sign of the organization that is necessary for such war.

Because of this there were no permanent war chiefs among the Pomo or their neighbors, though men of proven fighting and leadership ability generally took charge of any war action or expedition. The regular chiefs might come too or come later, but more often as peacemakers.

Wars might start because of bad-feeling over a trade, a reported poisoning, trespassing on another people's land without permission, stealing of women or children, and so on. Battles were of two kinds, open battles with two lines of men opposing each other, or sneak attacks, sometimes developing into massacres when a strong band of raiders attacked a sleeping village. Usually the open battle ended when an important man on one side or the other was killed or injured by a flying spear or arrow (these battles were usually at a distance with little close-quarter fighting). Generally the chiefs then arranged a payment for the loss and a settlement of the quarrel was made.

A rather more vicious battle than usual of this type took place about 1850 on Kelsey Creek in Lake County when the Lileek Miyakh'mah (or Wappo) joined with the Southeastern Pomo to battle with the Eastern Pomo over fishing rights to this creek. Ten men were killed in the fighting, which was won by the Eastern Pomo.

About 1830 a sneak-attack battle took place near the present town of Geyserville. The Mishewal of Pipolhoma (across the Russian River from Geyserville) had gathered a lot of acorns on their side of a boundary creek called Popeech, and left them overnight. The Pomo of the village of Ossokowi took the pile in the night. In reprisal, the Mishewal made two sudden and sneak attacks on Ossokowi, wiping out most of the village. A lot of land was given up by the Pomo because of this attack (see map).

Religion and Family Life.

General.

Religion and family life were tightly tied together in the Pomo culture. Though they believed in a Creator God, sometimes personalized by the figure of Coyote, or of Thunder (seen as a great bird with thundering wings and with lightning hidden under the wings), their daily religious life revolved around familiar spirits of fields and woods. These spirits existed in rocks and trees and other familiar objects or were ghosts that took the form of men, women or animals, or sometimes monsters. Most of them were evil, but, to avoid this evil, the Pomo had to carry out certain customs or actions, sing regular daily prayer songs, and not do certain things (taboos). Fear of these spirits and their actions had added to it fear of being poisoned by enemies, even some among their own people. We must realize that these fears were very real to these people, just as the fear of eternal fire is very real to some Christians.

In any case the Pomo faith in their religion was so strong that it did some very good things for them. It was probably one of the main reasons they washed daily and generally cleaned up all garbage and sewage. This was because they believed parts of this material, if found by an enemy, would be used to poison them. It also made lies and crime of the usual type almost totally unknown, for they feared what would happen to them if they lied or stole. It kept most men from chasing other men's wives, and there were very strict taboos against this. It made them keep care of all children with love and kindness, for the little ones were considered all part of the same big family. It made them protect the land and wildlife from too much exploitation (such as we have) as evil spirits attacked people who were too greedy about killing game or destroying trees, and so forth.

Marriages were often arranged by parents, but girls were rarely forced to marry men they did not like. Great prestige came to parents and families when a marriage was successful so care was often taken in choosing mates. Young men usually had to prove they could support a wife before they were allowed to marry. As among many California Indians, there was a taboo about talking to your mother-in-law, which probably helped cut down on quarrelling. Two strong families coming together in a marriage felt a sense of double protection, as all helped each other against dangerous outside forces, such as the poisoners.

Since most families in a tribelet or band were related in one way or another through marriages, there was a strong sense of cohesion in such a group. The chief and elders initiated the boys and girls into adulthood at certain ceremonies that must have been rather frightening experiences to the youngsters and included making a knife cut in the back. This highly dramatic experience emphasized to the youth the power of his elders and the need to obey them and to seek help from them against evil. If a boy, for example, became a cause of trouble in the community, tremendous pressure was brought to bear on him from both family and village leaders to change his ways. If he refused to obey, he could be banished completely from the village and from all association with other Pomo. This was very close to a sentence of death, as a Pomo without family and village connections could be attacked and killed by anybody without any protection. Few indeed in the old days allowed such a terrible thing to strike them.

The impact of the whites on Pomo culture often destroyed this power of the family and the village elders. Though becoming Christian helped bring something to replace this loss, it still did not have the unifying force of the old Pomo religion, and many Pomo became victims of alcoholism and other bad habits they learned from the worst class of whites. Fortunately, many Pomo today are seeing the need to revive pride and interest in the old culture and unity and to find a way to bring the young people back into the wonderful circle of cooperation many of the old native families and villages once had.

In the old days almost all the Pomo sang prayers by day and by night, prayers to strengthen themselves to face life and its troubles and yet be happy and strong. Some of the noblest of the Pomo used to climb the mountains and sing these songs and pray and fast until they were given a dream they believed came from the Great Spirit or His representative. Both men and women who did this often became healers and leaders.

The three main kinds of healers were the Sucking Doctors, the Herb and Magic Doctors, and the Kuksu Doctors. The latter healed only at the great Kuksu ceremonies. The Sucking Doctors professed to suck objects out of sick people and used a strong psychology to heal them. The Herb and Magic Doctors used healing herbs, also set bones, and had magic objects and songs that they used over a period of four days to effect healing. Since these doctors became successful only if they actually were able to heal people and many did well, they must have had ability.

The development and history of religious ideas.

In some Indian groups it is possible to trace back the origin of religious ideas to what we can call a culture hero, a man or woman of such tremendous spiritual power and vitality that he or she dramatically influenced the thinking of the people for centuries.   Such a one was Quetzalcoatl, the Feathered Serpent, of the Toltecs in Mexico, or Buffalo Maiden of the Sioux, who taught the people high ideals and to turn directly to the Spirit, without the need for too much taboo or intricate ceremony. In the Pomo we find traces of such a person in the way the chiefs and other religious leaders emphasized such qualities as chastity, truthfullness, trustworthiness, and cooperation, things always emphasized by the culture heroes. But we find no actual description of such a person unless it is possibly Kuksu (see below).

There is a possibility that the culture hero starts such high standards of honor, but they fall gradually into disrepair or, at least, are modified by human beings who have begun to neglect spiritual qualities for material.   It is possible that Kuksu, the hero god from the south, impersonated in the Kuksu ceremonies, was actually at one time a human being who taught a new religion to the natives of northern California. The signs of the decay in this religion are the appearance of the poisoners and the bear doctors in the Pomo religion.   The poisoners used the power of the fear they could inspire in the hearts of men by the poison-making rituals they practiced to control or injure them.   The poisoner rarely literally poisoned his victims, but rather made them think they were being poisoned. If he could obtain some nail parings of the one he wished to poison, for example, he could let the victim know he had these and was using them against him. Belief in this was so strong that people actually died from the fear and the sureness they felt of death coming.   A powerful family, however, was able to counteract this by prayers, songs, and by calling in a healing doctor who had the power to counteract the poisoner.

Bear impersonators appeared in some ceremonies, where they were harmless.   But other bear impersonators, called bear doctors, dressed in bear skins in the woods and were supposed to have power to travel very rapidly from place to place. They carried knives with them and would attack a lonely hunter or other single person in the forest, killing him and taking his money and weapons.   Or they might use the fear they inspired to blackmail people into doing things they wanted or paying them something they wanted. The chiefs usually tried to counter the bear doctors and the poisoners, and these men, when actually encountered by several Pomo, would likely be killed. So good struggled with evil among the Pomo as elsewhere. The mistake many missionaries made was to consider anything connected with the old Indian religion evil, not seeing or understanding how it gave the people a feeling of cultural unity and spiritual strength in a way that is vital to the balance, growth and maturity of individuals.

Whether a culture hero made the change or not, there seems to have been an apparent enrichment of the religion of northern California around a thousand years ago. Presumably then the Kuksu religion began to take form, probably first with the Wintun because of the complexity of its development with them. Before that these native peoples had a less complex religion (see page 51), including ghost worship, initiation ceremonies of the boys and girls into adulthood, the use of the bull-roarer to scare both youngsters and women into believing the older men were assisted by powerful spirits, the unspecialized healing of the sick and injured by medicine men and women and a direction of life by contact with the spirit world. The bull-roarer was an instrument swung rapidly through the air to produce a bull-like roar.

The spread of the Kuksu religion brought greater interaction between peoples because members of different linguistic groups crossed the boundaries to visit each others' ceremonies. The Kuksu and other ceremonies are too complex to describe here in detail, but the basic idea was a renewal of the spiritual life of the community, a taking away of the sins and ills, and an initiation of the young. In the Kuksu Ceremony men dressed up to act as impersonators of powerful spirits. Usually all men of the band or tribelet belonged to the Kuksu Society and took part in some way or another in the ceremonies that were held either in the sacred round house, or inside a circular brush fence in the summertime. A master of ceremonies directed the whole program, but there were other special officers, such as the head drummer, the fire-tender, and the head singer. More social dancers began the four days of the "big time", including dancing by women and mixed dances, but the Kuksu ceremonial dancing, which came later, was done entirely by men. The actual appearance of Kuksu and other head-impersonators, usually was preceded by the appearance of the "fire-devils" and other clown-like characters, who nevertheless had a very important part in the ceremony. These elaborately painted and usually naked men came running out of the woods to the ceremonial place, frightening women and children, throwing boys to be initiated through the fire, with special roughness for those who were considered bullies or otherwise delinquent, and appearing to eat or handle red-hot coals, which they might even toss at the spectators. They were finally chased away by other men, after what appeared to be quite a struggle and much to the relief of the weeping women and children.

Last came the true Kuksu Dancers, who danced in circles and turned their bodies in circles in symbolic harmony with the universe. The dancers often had breastplates and elaborate headdresses of woodpecker feathers, as well as long painted staffs with feathered tips. Sick people were brought forward to be healed by the impersonator of Kuksu, and the dancers going away into the woods at the end symbolized the taking away of all sickness and sin from the village.

In recent years the original Kuksu religion has become considerably modified by the coming of the Ghost Dance from Nevada, and the development of dreamers, particularly women, who claim direct connection with the Great Spirit, and have more or less combined the old religion with elements of Christianity. It has been called the Maru or Dreamer Cult.

Myths.

The Pomo had many beautiful and interesting myths. We have room here only for a condensed version of one called "The Creation of the Ocean" (as told by Herman James, August, 1957, and reprinted here by kind permission of the University of California Press, from KASHAYA TEXTS, by Robert Oswalt).

"Long ago Coyote was the smartest of all. He presided just like a heavenly being with his people. At that time there were no human beings, but the animal people talked.

"One time Coyote went off into the wilderness a long way. The land was burning hot as he went and without water. When he came to a large flat field, he was sick from thirst. Sitting down, resting on his knees, he looked as far as his eyes could see. Then he picked up a stick and dug with it to try to find water.

"Suddenly he began to see a little water where he was digging. He continued digging and then it suddenly spouted up high, as if it would never stop! Thereupon he ran away, not because he was afraid, but in order to see from a distance. From a small hill he soon saw that the land below was filled completely with water.

"At first he drank the water, but later it turned salty because it was the ocean. It had become bitter because of what we call ashes, so he called it 'bitter water', meaning ocean.

"In the beginning the water lay still just like a lake, but soon he took a stick and made the water move in waves, saying 'do like this! Make waves!' Then, when he had walked up the hill a little way, the water surged up in high waves, breaking way over the rocks. Then he scratched a mark to set the limits to which the water could go, which is why the ocean rises no farther. After he fixed the high limit of the tide, he scratched another mark to show how far the tide would go out.

"Then he prepared food in the ocean for people to gather. He knew that people were going to eat food when they became people, though, at first, they were animals.

"He threw down a big log and it became a whale. Then he threw down smaller logs he made live and they became seals and porpoises. He threw a dried manzanita bush into the sea and it became a swordfish. Soon all kinds of fish he was naming and throwing down.

"Then he cast down edible foods to grow on the rock, like abalones, mussels, goose barnacles, and bullheads that could be fished with a line from the rocks. And he said edible seaweed would grow on the rocks. He also put down limpets, small and large chitons, sea anemones, and so forth, missing nothing that people would need to eat.

"Then he created us Indians in the woods and gave us very healthy food to eat so our people never got sick but grew old and just died. They didn't have the sweet food the white men brought that makes us sick. "

We notice in many of these myths how animals are spoken of as if they were human beings, or at least were the ancestors of human beings. Essentially the Indians were expressing the belief that all living things were creations of the Great Spirit and should be treated with respect. Thus Indian children were taught to observe the actions of animals and birds with great closeness because they could learn lessons of how to live from such observations. In the instincts of the animals there was often great wisdom.

Pomo ceremonial rock in Knight's Valley 6 miles north of Hopland, 1904. Photo by Dr. Barrett, courtesy of Lowie Museum of Anthropology, University of California, Berkeley.

Pomo dance and ceremonial house, recent type, west of Geyserville, about 1900. Photo by P. M. Jones, courtesy of the Lowie Museum of Anthropology, Univ. of California, Berkeley.

DIVISION TWO - NEIGHBORS OF THE POMO

CHAPTER FIVE - YUKIAN-SPEAKING PEOPLES

(Note: Many Indian groups are called by names that are not actually their own. In the discussion following both the outsider-given name of the tribal group and its real name for itself are given when possible.)

NORTHERN YUKIAN-SPEAKING PEOPLES - YUKI, HUCHNOM AND COAST YUKI

The name Yuki comes from a neighboring people of the Penutian language family, the Wintun, with the meaning of "enemy." The Yukian-speaking peoples were, like the Pomo, divided into many tribelets or bands, and the local name of such a tribelet usually ended with the suffix "nom", meaning people. Thus Huchnom means "people out of the valley" because they lived in the canyon of the Eel River above the valley. The inland Yuki were divided into many tribelets or "noms", some of which are mentioned on page 61. The Coast Yuki called themselves by the rather unusual name of "Ukoht-ontilka", which means "beside the big water."

All three of these groups of people had less material goods than the Pomo because they lived in more hilly country with less easily-available food and other material resources. We can think of them as being mountaineers or hill men, with more difficulties to face in life, and so probably hardier and more aggressive than the Pomo. Nevertheless, their culture was distinctive and beautiful in their own minds. The Yuki were very good friends to the Northeastern Pomo of Stony Creek, although they sometimes fought with the Northern Pomo.

The culture and nature of these Yukian-speaking peoples was, in many ways, similar to that of the Pomo, as we have already discussed it, but there were some interesting differences that help make them stand out as a distinct group of peoples.

1. Most striking was the way they looked. They were a very short people, the men averaging about 5 foot 2 1/2 inches and the women around 5 feet. They had unusually narrow heads for California natives and also had broader noses than any of their neighbors. It is very strange that the similar-speaking Wappo (or Miyahkmah) look very much like the Pomo. Having a similar language does not necessarily mean having similar looks.

2. The Yuki had much more twined than coiled basketry and had simpler decorations than the Pomo, though beautiful. They used dogwood mainly for the foundation rather than willow, and redbud was generally used for the sewing instead of sedge root. For white in the pattern the inner side of the redbud was used, and the outer side was used for red. Soaked bark made black. This was in coiled baskets. In twined baskets both the warp and weft were generally made of willow. In coiled baskets the Yuki worked from right to left, the Pomo from left to right.

3. Yuki women wore basket hats, seldom worn by the Pomo.

4. The Yuki did not have as many or as elaborate dance costumes as did the Pomo.

5. The Yuki were more typical of the old California type general culture, as they had absorbed little of the Kuksu Religion, with its elaborate ceremonials, and put more emphasis on initiation ceremonies and training schools for boys and girls. They also partook somewhat of ceremonies connected with ghosts of once living people, a phenomena common to the old native California religion of the centuries before the appearance of Kuksu and his religion. The ghosts appeared in dances, especially to help initiate the boys into manhood.

6. The Yuki had less specialization in forms of work. Thus men were usually both fishers and hunters, not just one alone.

The Coast Yuki had a material culture close to that of the coastal Pomo, as both depended mainly on sea food for a livelihood.

SOUTHERN YUKIAN-SPEAKING PEOPLE - THE WAPPO or MIYAHKMAH

The name Wappo is said to be an Americanized version of a Spanish word "guapo", meaning "warrior." The Wappo were given this name by the Californianos of the Sonoma Mission and General Vallejo's company because they showed considerable bravery and military ability in ambushing and sometimes even defeating soldiers brought against them by Salvador Vallejo, the brother of General Mariano Vallejo. They were clever at concealing themselves in the brush.

The Wappo were divided into three major divisions, the Mishewal, the Mitustil and the Miyahkmah, which last name is probably the best native name for the whole group. A small offshoot of the first division, called the Lileek, moved, a hundred and fifty years or so ago, up to the southern edge of Clear Lake (see page 40).

The Miyahkmah ordinarily were a hill people, less elaborate in material culture than the Pomo but proud of their hardy self-reliance. Usually they got along quite well with the Pomo, however, doing much trading with them, even joining them in ceremonial dances, and were generally allowed by the Pomo to go down to the sea through Pomo territory, bringing back dried seaweed, fish and other marine products.

Since the Miyahkmah were right in the middle between the two populous and prosperous language groups, the Pomo on the west and the Wintun on the east, they naturally absorbed much of their culture, including the Kuksu Religion, the complex and beautiful basketry, and some of the specializations in work, such as the making of magnesite money. There were a few distinctive differences, however, as follows :

1. They had few luxuries of dress, such as head-nets for women, or seal or otter-skin robes for chiefs and other head men, and did not use tattooing as did some of the Pomo.

2. At the time a woman had a baby the couvade was put into practice, meaning the husband would lie in bed as if he were the one having the baby.

3. Fishing was done without the fish hooks, dip nets and gill nets generally used by the Pomo.

4. No brush deer nets or blinds were used to trap deer as done by the Pomo.

5. Ritual and taboos surrounding hunting were much less than among neighboring peoples.

6. No plank drum was used in the dance house, just rattles.

7. Rabbitskin blankets and capes of tule were woven between two poles using a horizontal warp instead of vertical as with the Pomo.

8. The Miyahkmah did not believe in were-bears as did the Pomo, nor did they try to cure a man frightened by a ghost by frightening him again. But they did believe poisoners could travel rapidly over the land at night.

9. They had puberty ceremonies for girls, but not for boys.

10. Women desiring babies went to a certain rock near Geyser Spring to pray, as this rock had hand and foot prints of a baby carved on it, supposedly by spirits.

11. The whole wing of an eagle was worn in the hair of certain brave warriors in war.

12. Coyote was supposed to create people out of feathers, but Old Man Moon had to supply the special powers of breathing, talking and walking, according to Miyahkmah legend.

CHAPTER SIX - MIWOK-SPEAKING PEOPLE

THE TULEYOME

The Lake Miwok or Tuleyome, as they called themselves, were an almost-destroyed group by the time the first educated white men began to investigate the native peoples. This made them almost miss recognition as a people. Not long ago, when one of the authors of this book visited the area and talked to a descendant of the Tuleyome, a woman, she first claimed to be a Pomo, but, when she began to name the old native villages of the area and explain the meanings of the names, it became clear that she was a Tuleyome and not a Pomo. There is an unusual liquid lilt to the sound of names when spoken by the Miwok-speaking peoples. From the Sierra Nevada, for example, we have such beautiful water-splashing sounds as Tuolumne (Tu-wol-ohm-nay), Wawona (Wah-wo-nah), and Illilouette (Illil-ouw-yet). A look on the map of our area around the lower end of Clear Lake will disclose similar lovely-sounding names. In all, the most beautiful-sounding words for place names in California would seem to come from the Indians.

We know little about the early culture of the Tuleyome beyond the fact that they probably had most of the material, social and religious culture of their neighbors. One of their legends states that the village of Tuleyome was where Coyote, the creator, came to make the world.

THE OLAMENTKO AND HUKUEKO

The so-called Coast Miwok were divided into the Olamentko of the Bodega Bay Area and the Hukueko of the bulk of Marin County and the Petaluma area of Sonoma County (see map). The Hukueko were probably the first northern California Indians ever to be seen by white men. In 1579 Sir Francis Drake landed somewhere on the shore of what is now Marin County and encountered the Hukueko, whom he found very friendly and cooperative, as were almost all California natives when they first met the white people. The English were astonished at the strength shown by the Hukueko in carrying 200 pound loads, but decided that the sinew-backed bow of the Indians was only a toy compared to the powerful English yew long bow.

Both Olamentko and Hukueko were similar in culture to the Pomo, though less complicated in some aspects, such as in their basketry, which was mostly coiled and included little that was twined. Since the Washington Clam was very abundant in the Bodega Bay area where the Olamentko had many villages, these people traded these "money" clams to the Pomo and others for skins, sinew-backed bows and many other trading items. The Pomo, who, with these clams, were the chief money-manufacturers, traded back their money beads for more clams.

Bodega Head, the long finger of land that protects Bodega Bay from the sea, is a rich source of Indian artifacts that goes back many centuries, showing a gradually increasing complexity of tools down through the years, including fish-hooks of exquisite workmanship, made out of abalone shells. Mrs. Rose Gaffney of Bodega has made an amazing collection of these artifacts.

The earth oven of the Olamentko and Hukueko was perhaps a bit more elaborate than that of the Pomo, so this way of cooking is worth explaining here. A three to four feet deep pit was dug (see page 25) in clayey ground, its bottom and sides lined with stones, pushed in on the sides to hold them against the clay. A fire was built in the hole and kept burning until the stones were extremely hot. Next the upper part of the fire was removed, leaving some hot coals on the bottom, and the hole filled with first a layer of clover and then a layer of hot stone, making several layers in this way. Large leaves were put above this, and then layers of dirt. When the clover was thoroughly cooked, it was then dried and kept stored as an emergency food. While bread could be baked in this oven, the most delicious meals imaginable were cooked by lowering a rough basket or lattice of meat, tubers and greens into a nest of green leaves placed over red hot coals and stones, more leaves and hot stones placed on top and the whole covered with hard-tamped earth, then left for about four hours. If properly done, meat and vegetables came out of the earth so tender and delicious that they melted in the mouth, as at least one of the authors has found by experience.

Both Hukueko and Olamentko possibly were related to the people who left signs of a many-thousand year occupancy of the land by the great shell mounds found along the shores of the bays. It is obvious that these mounds mark the presence of villages that were permanent fixtures for tens of centuries, and where people made the most of their living from marine life, unlike the majority of the people we have so far discussed. These great shell and refuse mounds are archaeological treasure grounds for discarded tools, beads and other artifacts.

CHAPTER FIVE - PATWIN AND NOMLAKI WINTUN

All along the west side of the Sacramento Valley and extending up to the crest of the Coast Range (except for the little Pomo colony on Stony Creek) were the Wintun-speaking people of the Penutian Language Family. North of the Stony Creek Pomo they were called the Wintun or Nomlaki, and south they were called the Patwin. These were each divided into the hill tribelets, who bordered the Pomo, and the valley tribelets, who lived down near the big river. The latter, of course, had the more complex culture because they lived in land filled with a plentiful food supply. But it is with the hill people that we deal here.

Somewhere in Wintun territory, some scientists believe, was the most likely beginning of the Kuksu Cult, which spread widely throughout north central California in recent centuries. We have discussed this religion briefly (see pages 45-46), but the Wintun have revived it in modern times in the form called the Big Head Cult. C. Hart Merriam, a California ethnologist, has described this dance, a short summary of which we give here.

The Big Head Dance combines ghost, dream and war dances and the dancers show scenes from the dream of a famous medicine man. The fantastic costumes show the dancers' heads covered with large caps or mats from which point upward long slender willow sticks decorated with many lovely flowers and tipped with white feathers. The inner bark of the maple is shredded to make the kilt, which sways and ripples with the slightest movement of the dancers. Gorgeous red and yellow feathers of the flicker and the giant pileated woodpecker hang like ribbons from the belt. These are the Big Head dancers and they perform in pairs, each dancer holding a clapper stick, which they shake exactly in time to the dance steps.

Soon there enters the Red Cap, a woman who dances to represent the old woman witch or war goddess. She has a huge red mask covering most of her head and peers from under it while lifting and waving a brilliantly striped bow in one hand in perfect time to the singers and dancing. She is soon followed by a young man, crowned with yellow flicker feathers and having a quiver of fox skin full of arrows. Dexterously he dances backward and forward, urged on by the goddess to become a warrior. The beautiful, soft and low-voiced songs, the amazing dancing, the dark faces flashing in the firelight are indeed most impressive and thrilling, a sign of the Indian spirit. *

---

* Adapted from STUDIES OF CALIFORNIA INDIANS, by C. Hart Merriam. 1962. Univ. of California Press. Pages 27-28. With permission of the publishers.

Such dances often last all night, and are followed by a big feast in the morning, then sleep. The excitement of these big times is probably greater than our own circuses, and much more human-involving since most of the people took part in some way.

The great length of Wintun territory, from the Sacramento River marshes up to Trinity and Siskiyou Counties in the north, probably made for a great variety of culture. The Nomlaki Wintun and Patwin Wintun, who were nearest the Pomo, were a hill people with a less complicated or material-rich culture than their relatives in the Great Valley or the Clear Lake Pomo.

The following are some distinctive features.

1. There was some ornamentation of the breast and stomach with tattoo-markings.

2. Most large counting was done in 80's, and it is possible that 4 was considered the basic number.

3. Unlike the Pomo, who used cremation, most of the Wintun buried their dead. The body was often put in a hunched position, wrapped with strings of shell money and then with a skin, such as a bear skin. It was dropped into a shallow grave dug with sticks and undercut to the west side, so that the body came to rest as if in a cave. Property was buried with the dead among the Patwin, but usually burned a month later among the Nomlaki. This destruction or burying of property at or after the time of death was sentimental, and not connected directly with a desire to give something for the dead to take with them. It should be pointed out here that most California Indians did not mention the name of a dead relative nor expect others to.

4. The shamans or medicine men used special spirits, the clouds, stars and sun giving powers for good, while the wolf, dog and sucker were supposed to be used for evil.

5. The chief god or creator was called Olelbis, meaning "he who is above."

6. The Patwin seem to have had the most elaborate manifestation of the Kuksu cult or religion, with as many as twelve different grades of initiates in the society, something like our modern Masons, with their several degrees. Those of the highest degrees had special tasks and privileges. They were usually called the "Moki", and did the highest impersonations of spirits. Some spirits men were afraid to impersonate unless they were taught how to do it by a close relative.

A. PLACE NAMES AND THEIR MEANINGS

Most of the names given on our map are taken from Dr. S. A. Barrett's book on THE ETHNOLOGY OF THE POMO, Univ. of Calif. Publ. in American Archaeology and Ethnology, Volume 6, Map 1. The meanings of the names are taken from this book and also from several modern Indians, to whom we are deeply appreciative, Mrs. Elsie Allen of Ukiah, Mrs. Essie Parrish of Stewart's Point, and Mr. Ralph Holder of Upper Lake, Pomo, and Mrs. Doris Yee, Tuleyome of Middletown. The pronunciation of these names is often very difficult and Dr. Barrett was not a linguist. However, due to the many variations of dialect, the Indians themselves often disagree on pronunciation and spelling. In some places we put more than one name for a village on our list. Meanings of names are given where we have been able to find them. Main villages are underlined where known, and groups of villages connected with them put under the name of each main village.

(Note that each political unit of the Pomo has a grey line around it.)

POMO VILLAGE NAMES

SOUTHWESTERN POMO (Kah-chi-ah)

Danága (cover-up point)
Ouwimatcaéli
Ohomtol (nettle place)
Kapácinal (bracken head)

Chitíbidakali
Tabatéwi (on big beach)
Sulmewi (rope place)
Ótonoe (purple seaweed)
Kabesiláwina (upon flat rock)
Tcítono

Meténi or Chwachamaja (part of
a place)
Bacéyokaili (under buckeye water)
Powicana (red clay ridge)

Chalánchawi
Kalemálato (around a tree)
Tcamúka
Tsútkanitcanawi
Katáka (woodpecker place)
Tsubátcemali (flat hole bush place)
Acatcátiu (fish house)
Kabémali (rock there place)

Hibúwi (Indian potato place)
Mutcáwi (grass seed place)
Atcaninatcáwalli (head of man
sitting down place)
Tsununu-Shinal (present site of
Kashia Rancheria, Stewart's Point)

Kalecádim (tree on little ridge)
Tádono (bird mountain)

Tcalámkiamali (to wind around a
place on both sides)
Tátcumawali (place where food is
set off the ground)
Lálaka (wild goose spring)
Kabotcitcákali (narrow open strip of
land with grass on it place)

Potol (red spring dance house here)
Matíwi (at the wild oats)
Malkabel

Seepínamatci (see brush far away)
Tanám
Kaletcúmaial (sitting under a tree)
Tsapúwil (acorn-shaped)

SOUTHERN POMO (Mah-kah-mo-chum)

Makáhmo (Sulphur Lake)
Gatctíyo   Amáko (dirt field)
Akámotcolowani
Kalánko
Motitcáton (rattlesnake house)

Cawáko or Shawáko (Mishewal Wappo
called this village "Walnut'tse",
meaning "little warriors").
Kiwiñkwitiman

Wotokkáton (dirty ashes lake). Chief
of this village was known as Man-
ka or Soto (a Miwok word). Many
converts for the Sonoma Mission
were taken from here (called So-
toyome by Spaniards).
Takókalewi
Catcáli

(Wotokkáton group continued.)
Kabéton (under rock)
Amascatcílan
Watakkówi (frog water village)
Bacáklekau (broken buckeye tree)
Mukakotcáli (ant village), some
fighting with Mishewal took
place here about 1834.
Lúli
Kále (water place)
Cútakowi
Bakátsio
Hélwamécon
Kawámio (under pine ground)
Yocíkletowani (stand up white
oak tree)

Kábekadogani
Úpawani
Amatío
Bidutsákaleyo
Makásmo
Amalpuwóli
Kolóko
Kátowi (lake place), famous in old
times for mysterious log that
carried people about the lake and
Frog Woman who bellowed at night.
Djópten
Káwikawi
Heéman

Catýinen
Behekáuna
Kalátken
Délema
Búdutcilan
Baọaklenónan (buckeye tree)
Tsíwada
Tsolikáwi
Hatcílon
Úpawani
Ciohutmokóni

Tcétcewani
Butswáli
Kápten
Cakákmo
Tciléton
Kacíntui
Masikáwani

Wílok
Kabetciuwa

Hukabetyáwi
Cutáwani
Tóhmakau

Batíklechawi (alder tree house)
Akapólopolowani
Bútakatcatakani
Bóhosole

Katsanosma (grass ashes sleep)
Kabétewi (big rock place)
Dówikaton (under coyote springs)
Takóton
Káhowani (near hot water), location
at Skagg's Springs

Hiwalhmu (point where 2 springs meet)
Duwíditem
Bímukaton
Búlakowi
Máhmo
Kawamtcáeli

Shámli or Cámli
Kobáte
Mákawina (salmon ridge)
Kawantélimani (flat-head pine)

Kubahmói
Kabetéyo

Kowíshal or Kowícal (mussel-ridge)
Kalínda (steep place trail)
Tcápida
Seéton (where brush grows)
Kabuputcémali (madrone stand-up-
straight place)

CENTRAL POMO (Yokiah-Boyah)

Kolóko

Cépda
Kcákaleyo
Mákatcam

Káhwalau
Kabéyo (under rock village)
Yótceuk (south corner)
Iwída (coyote trail)
Cósamal

Canél (sweat house)
Kawíaka (small water)
Kawímo (small hole)

Ciégo (grass seed valley)
Silala (between redwoods)

Tátem (sandy small open space)

Múyamuya (strange being or hairy man giant), a giant nine to ten feet high was supposed to live here.

Tcákca (house canyon village)

Léma (between or low down place)

Húkdia (strange bird place)

Shókadjat or Cókadjal

Canémilam (burned sweathouse)

Bókca (west canyon)

Bodono (west mountain)

Canéneu (to place the sweat house)

Láli

Notcétiyo   Kaiyélle

Mabóton

Láte

Kaláicolem

Ctála

Kóthwi

Sánalyo

Dakólkabe (rock pestle place)

Látcupda

Katsáiwani

Iwíkbedabau (split with the hand of coyote rock)

Mátasama (near red ground)

Mácanena (on top of ground sweathouse place)

Klétel (peel off tree)

Tcámsumli (burned house there)

Pdáhau (river mouth)

Djécomi

Kódalau

Damáldau

Káuca

Kasíltcimada (redwood run up stream)

Nákoca

NORTHERN POMO (Me-tum-mah)

Kadíu

Yákale

Nóyo

Djómo

Gaiyetíl

Kabétsitu

Búldam (flat rock)

Tcádam

Ditcólel

Kaláili

Kabátoda

Tcaida

Húda

Tcúlgo (north valley village)

Kátuuli (old water place)

Djómi

Tábate (big sand)

Nópik

Cómda

Kabédjal (rock house)

Cúnaubasatnapotai (pretty forks old village)

Lemkólil

Kalémsupda (tree burned creek place)

Kabéela

Kacímdalau

Matô (big village)

Kabédile (amid rocks)

Káikitsil (end of valley)

Bikeká (ground squirrel water)

Kabótsui (clover corner)

Mátcata (between ground)

Tanacíl (hang down hand)

Bócamkutci (see moss place)

Tsikinídano (owl mountain)

Kaáika (water crow)

Kamádokai (cold water valley)

Behémkalum (bay wood gone)

Sósatca (red ant house)

Canémko (scorched sweat house)

Kulákai (yellow water lily valley)

Kabédano (rock mountain)

Butáka (bear village)

Tíkai (string village)

Cakókai (willow valley)

Bakáu
Kabéyo (under rock village)
Yami

Tsamómda
Tsaká (smoke village)

Cotsiu (east corner)
Mitóma (yearly hanging grapevine)
Katakal (hollow mussel)
Kabecál
Behépata (pound bay tree nuts)
Kótsiyu
Kacaidámal
Hodudúkawe (built like king snake)

Bitádanek
Cabákana
Tanakóm (hand bog)
Kóbida (madrone flat village)

Káshake or Kátcake

Dapishu
Katcábida
Kabelál

Masút

Chómchadila or Tcómtcadila (pitch
    pine people village or cone of
    bull pine extends down).
Cimákau or Cimákawi

Kómli (soda spring there)
Cókadjal or Kókatcal
Kátili
Kabegílnal
Sméwakapda (wolf water creek)
Tcidotéya

Shachámkau or Catcámkau or
    Tcámkaui

Tsakámo (smoke hole)
Matuku (cold creek)

Pómo (red earth people)
Kalálpicul
Katcábida

Sédam
Kalésima

Shanél or Canél
Motítca (house in a hole)
Yámo
Sótca or Bata'ka

Canékai (sweat house valley)
Tisyákabeyo

Mayi
Hómtcati (nettle place)
Mamámamou (projecting point)
Xaró (baked black bread)

Nobóral (on mud ashes)
Samákahna
Síwaklal
Káraka (dry limb filled with wood-
    pecker holes and water)

EASTERN POMO (Hah-nah-bah)

Xówalek or Howalek

Yóbutui (south knoll)
Kucádonoyo (live oak mountain)

Danóxa or Danóha (mountain water)
Danoco (east Mountain)
Badónnapoti (old island)
Ciwá (bird village)
Kakúlkalewical (white oak tree ridge)
Láxputsum (inlet point)
Diwílem (coyote flat)
Behépal (laurel or peppernut village)

Shigom (here we are)
Hálika (laurel nut flesh)
Taáwina (upon sand)

Kashíbadon (water plant island)
Boomli (to hunt around)
Katótnapoti (old laurel nut shell)

Bidámiwina (close to creek)
Cabégok (rocks sticking up)
Hmarágimowina (on top of dance
    house hole)
Nónapoti (old ashes village)

SOUTHEASTERN POMO (Ham-fo)

Kámdot
Cákai
Kécelwai (shooting out blue clay)
Ktsúkawaᴅ (under oak tree ball)
Tciyólkitlali

Elém
Kiyéutsit

Koi
Kuúlbidae (ridge where water comes
Xubé   /out

NORTHEASTERN POMO(Sho-té-ah)

Bakámtati
Túrururaibida
Amótati
Odílaka
Duhultamtíwa
Mihiltamtíwa

Cheétido
Kakoskál
Tátaca
Katákto

OTHER TRIBAL NAMES
(alphabetically arranged)

COAST YUKI (Ukoht-ontilka)

Bidáto (mush river)

YUKI PROPER (Hutc-nom)

Hunkalítc
Ywuluíme

(Note: the Yuki were called Hutc-nom or "mountain people" along South Eel River and Outlet Creek; Yek-mal-nom or "Yek Creek People" near Traveler's Home; On-kel-ukomnom, or \"Land-on-the-other-side-of-the-valley-people" in Gravelly Valley near Hulville; and Iwil-han-nom, or "Sweat-house people" in the valley of Stony Creek above Stonyford.)

HUCHNOM (also called Tatu or Redwoods People)

Cípomul   Baáwel
Hátupokai
Komomemutkuyúk
Lílkool
Mot
Mótkuyuk
Mumemét
Múpan (bunch of grapes)
Vonhohou
  ːkémul
  umnanoom
  ːk

WAPPO or MAYAHKMAH

Acáben (Pomo name of village)
Címela
Gaiyétcin (manzanita-hang-down)
Kolóko (long mortar basket village), a Pomo name
Kóticomota (black oak hill)
Loknóma (goose village)
Maiyákma
Malalatcóli (mosquito village), a Pomo name.
Mútistul
Níhlektsonoma
Pétinoma
Pipohólma (white oak tree grove) Took part in war against Pomo to south of them.
Tekenántsonoma (deep hole with mineral water)
Tsélmenan (deep hole with charcoal water)
Uyúhanoma
Wílikos (Coast Miwok name)

COAST MIWOK

HUKUEKO

Kótati
Susúli
Túlme

OLAMENTKO

Awachi
Éwapait
Helapáttai
Hime-tákala
Hotákala
Kénnekono
Lumentúkala
Oyéyomi (coyote home)
Pakáhuwe
Payinécha
Patawa-yomi
Pulya-Lakum
Súwutenne
Tíwut-huya
Témblek
Tókau (bird bone whistle)
Tulí
Ulíyomi

LAKE MIWOK or TULEYOME

Káwiyome (move down home)
Oléyome (coyote home)
Tsítsapogut (flint place home)
Túleyome (deep home)
Tumístumis

(Note: the meanings of the above village names show that the Tule-yome, like most California Indians, had a deep attachment for the places they lived in. In fact every rock and tree had a special meaning. Túle-yome was deeply woven into their legends as the center from which the earth was born, and may have a history going back through many thousands of years.)

WINTUN-SPEAKING PEOPLE

NOMLAKI WINTUN

Caípetel
Dátcimtcimi
Tóba
Tolókai

PATWIN WINTUN

Hólokome
Kulá or Kulálabe
Micháwish or Mitcáwiclabe
Pukúm or Pukúmlabe
Táwaisak
Téhti or Tébti
Tókti
Úlak

If we think things through, we can well imagine that the Indians actually went through far more pain and upset when they saw their villages set on fire by the white invaders than we would under similar circumstances. We late-comers to this land casually move every few years to new locations, rarely feeling the deep pangs the Indian felt at being separated from earth and tree and hill that sang in his heart and those of his ancestors for more centuries than we can ever truly understand!

SOME ODD POMO NAMES OF INTEREST

Chebal-no-Pomo or Chedil-na-Pomo (Pomo of the north country).
Huk (a mythical bird of evil whose quills carried inside them a poisonous red liquid that killed people).
Kanaktai (old woman mountain), the mountain just south of Clear Lake.
Kaptuton (deep pool on the Russian River where the boundary lies betweer the Central and the South Pomo).
Kitsidano (Bald Mountain).
Knotaiknowyoa (under old woman mountain), cliffs on east side of Mt. Kan-aktai.
Xádalam (water dam village), supposed to be somewhere on Kelsey Creek south of Clear Lake. At this place approximately 4000 Indians came in 1870 to dance the Ghost Dance in underground dance houses and wait for the big wind which was to destroy the white people and bring back the good days of old. Can we understand their longing?

SUGGESTED REFERENCES

Aginsky, B. W. and E. G. DEEP VALLEY. 1967 Stein and Day. A fictionalized recreation of Pomo life by two anthropologists.

Barrett, S. A. CEREMONIES OF THE POMO INDIANS. 1917. University of Calif. Publ. in Am. Arch. and Ethn., Vol. 2, No. 4.
- THE ETHNO-GEOGRAPHY OF THE POMO AND NEIGHBORING INDIANS. 1908. Univ. of Calif. Publ. in Am. Arch. and Ethn. Vol. 6, No. 1.
- THE GEOGRAPHY AND DIALECTS OF THE MIWOK INDIANS. 1908. U. C. Publ. in Am. Arch. and Ethn., Vol. 6, No. 2.
- MATERIAL ASPECTS OF POMO CULTURE. 1952. Bulletin of the Public Museum of the City of Milwaukee, Vol. 20, parts 1 & 2.
- POMO INDIAN BASKETRY. 1908. U. C. Publ. in Am. Arch. and Ethn., Vol. 7, No. 3.
- POMO BEAR DOCTORS. 1917. U. C. Publ. in Am. Arch. and Ethn., Vol. 12, No. 11.

Driver, Harold E. WAPPO ETHNOGRAPHY. 1936. U. C. Publ. in Am. Arch. and Ethn., Vol. 36, No. 3.

Dubois, C. WINTU ETHNOGRAPHY. 1935. U. C. Publ. in Am. Arch. and Ethno., Vol. 36, No. 1.

Gifford, E. W. POMO LANDS ON CLEAR LAKE. 1923. U. C. Publ. in Am. Arch. and Ethn., Vol. 20, No. 5.
- CLEAR LAKE POMO SOCIETY. 1926. U. C. Publ. in Am. Arch. and Ethn., Vol. 18, No. 2.

Heizer, R. F. and Whipple M. A. THE CALIFORNIA INDIANS - A Source Book. 1967. Univ. of Calif. Press.

Kniffen, Fred. POMO GEOGRAPHY. 1939. U. C. Publ. in Am. Arch. and Ethn., Vol. 36, No. 6.

Kroeber, A. L. CALIFORNIA KINSHIP SYSTEMS. 1917. U. C. Publ. in Am. Arch. and Ethn., Vol. 12, No. 9.
- ELEMENTS OF CULTURE IN NATIVE CALIFORNIA. 1922. U. C. Publ. in Am. Arch. and Ethn., Vol. 13, No. 8.
- HANDBOOK OF THE INDIANS OF CALIFORNIA. 1953. California Book Co, Ltd., Berkeley, Calif.
- THE PATWIN AND THEIR NEIGHBORS. 1932. U. C. Publ. in Am. Arch. and Ethn., Vol. 29, No. 4.

Loeb, E. M. POMO FOLKWAYS. 1926. U. C. Publ. in Am. Arch. and Ethn., Vol. 19, No. 2.
- THE WESTERN KUKSU CULT. 1932. U. C. Publ. in Am. Arch. and Ethn., Vol. 33, No. 1.
- THE EASTERN KUKSU CULT. 1933. U. C. Publ. in Am. Arch. and Ethn., Vol. 33, No. 2.

Merriam, C. Hart. STUDIES OF CALIFORNIA INDIANS. 1962. Univ. of California Press.

McKern, W. C. PATWIN HOUSES. 1923. U. C. Publ. in Am. Arch. and Ethn., Vol. 20, No. 10

Stewart, O. C. NOTES ON POMO ETHNOGRAPHY. 1943. U. C. Publ. in Am. Arch. and Ethn., Vol. 40, No. 2.

INDEX